TORTOLA

TRAVEL GUIDE

2025

Your complete insider manual for experiencing the best and discovering the hidden gems of this Paradise in British Virgin Islands

Copyright © 2024 [Jack Armstrong]

All rights reserved. No part of this publication may be reproduced, distributed, or transmitted in any form or by any means, including photocopying, recording, or other electronic or mechanical methods, without the prior written permission of the publisher, except in the case of brief quotations embodied in critical reviews and certain other noncommercial uses permitted by copyright law.

TABLE OF CONTENTS

Introduction: Overview of Tortola 7

    Introduction to Tortola 7

    Geography and Climate 9

    Best Times to Visit 11

Chapter 1. Brief History and Culture 13

    Historical Background 13

    Local Traditions and Customs 16

    Language and Religion 19

Chapter 2. Health and Safety Considerations 22

    Health Care Services 22

    Vaccination Requirements 24

    Safety Tips for Travelers 26

Chapter 3. Currency, Payment Methods, and Tipping 29

Local Currency and Payment Methods 29

Payment Methods (Credit Cards and Cash) 30

Tipping Etiquette 32

Chapter 4. How to Reach Tortola 33

International Flights and Airports 33

Ferry and Boat Services... 35

Entry Requirements (Visas, Customs) 37

Chapter 5. Transportation Options 39

Getting Around Tortola 39

Driving Tips and Road Conditions........................ 41

Ferries and Inter-Island Transportation 43

Chapter 6. Accommodations 46

Best Resorts and Hotels... 46

Budget-Friendly Stays 55

Chapter 7. Cuisine and Dining 59

    Must-Try Dishes and Drinks 59

    Best Restaurants and Local Eateries 62

Chapter 8. Practical Information 67

    Emergency Contacts and Medical Services 67

    Internet, Mobile Connectivity, and SIM Cards 69

    Local Laws and Etiquette 71

    Language Tips for Travelers 73

Chapter 9. Must-See Attractions 76

    Cane Garden Bay 76

    Smuggler's Cove 80

    Sage Mountain National Park 85

    Road Town (Capital City Highlights) 90

    Brewer's Bay 94

Chapter 10. Activities and Adventures 100

Snorkeling and Diving Spots 100

Boating, Sailing, and Yachting 102

Hiking Trails and Nature Walks 105

Water Sports (Kayaking, Paddleboarding) 108

Chapter 11. Shopping and Local Markets 111

Souvenir Shops and Local Crafts 111

Popular Markets for Local Goods 113

Chapter 12. Sample Itineraries 116

Family-Friendly Itinerary (3-5 Days) 116

Adventure Seeker's Itinerary (3-5 Days) 119

Cultural and Historical Itinerary (3-5 Days) 123

Conclusion 127

Final Thoughts 127

Introduction: Overview of Tortola

Introduction to Tortola

Tortola, the shining star of the British Virgin Islands, is like the best-kept secret you didn't know you were waiting to discover. Imagine a place where the ocean's many shades of blue meet lush green mountains and sun-kissed beaches, where the rhythm of island life hums to a melody of steel drums and the occasional wave crashing onshore. Sounds dreamy, right? Tortola is the perfect blend of laid-back island vibes with just enough adventure to keep your heart racing — and it's waiting to welcome you with open arms.

Whether you're a beach bum, a history buff, a sailor at heart, or a family looking to make unforgettable memories, Tortola has something for everyone. The island is big enough to explore for days yet small enough that you'll feel like a local in no time. With a backdrop of swaying palm trees, colorful houses, and friendly locals ready to chat, Tortola is an island that instantly feels like home — or at least the tropical home you never knew you needed!

And let's not forget the legendary pirate tales — yes, you're stepping into Blackbeard's old stomping grounds! The island is brimming with history, though these days, instead of treasure chests and hidden loot, you'll be hunting for sun, fun, and maybe the best rum punch you've ever had. Tortola will have you hooked, and once you experience its charm, you may find yourself plotting a return trip before you even leave.

Geography and Climate

Tortola is more than just its postcard-perfect beaches (although, let's be honest, those alone could win you over). It's a mountainous island, stretching about 13 miles long and 3 miles wide, with peaks that soar high above the turquoise waters below. Its rugged hills are covered in dense, tropical vegetation, making it a haven for hikers and nature lovers. Sage Mountain, the island's highest point, gives you a breathtaking panorama of both Tortola and the neighboring islands — a view that's worth every step of the climb.

The coastline is a mix of hidden coves, serene bays, and coral reefs teeming with marine life. It's the kind of place where you can spend one afternoon sunbathing on a secluded beach like Smuggler's Cove, and the next exploring the vibrant coral reefs just offshore. Inland, winding roads take you through sleepy villages, where pastel-colored houses dot the hillsides, and goats casually cross the street like they own the place (spoiler alert: they do).

As for the climate, Tortola is a Caribbean paradise, meaning it's warm and sunny nearly all year round. The temperature hovers between a pleasant 77°F and 88°F, with a gentle breeze to keep things comfortable. Expect a tropical climate, with a dry season from December to April — the perfect time to escape any winter blues back home. The rainy season, from May to November, brings occasional showers, but fear not: the rain often passes quickly, leaving the island even more vibrant and refreshed.

Just make sure to pack your sunscreen and a light rain jacket — and remember, any rain in paradise is just a brief pause in the fun! With its stunning landscapes and welcoming weather, Tortola's geography and climate set the stage for the ultimate island escape.

Best Times to Visit

When is the best time to visit Tortola, you ask? Well, the simple answer is: anytime! But let's break it down so you can plan your escape to paradise like a pro.

The sweet spot for most travelers is between **December and April**. This is Tortola's dry season, a magical time when the skies are blue, the breezes are gentle, and the sun practically begs you to kick back on the beach with a cold drink in hand. Plus, if you're coming from somewhere frosty, nothing feels better than trading snowflakes for sand between your toes. The days are warm, usually around a perfect 80°F (27°C), and the nights are comfortably cool — ideal for those romantic sunset dinners by the water. Just know this is also peak season, so you'll be sharing paradise with fellow sun-seekers (but hey, more people means more fun, right?).

If you're looking to dodge the crowds and save a few bucks, **May through November** offers a quieter, more laid-back vibe. This is Tortola's off-season, with fewer tourists and plenty of space on the beaches. Sure, it's the rainy season, but think of the rain as a refreshing island rinse that only lasts for a short while. The lush hillsides become even more vibrant, and everything smells fresh — plus, let's face it, a quick tropical shower never ruined a rum punch!

Just be aware that **hurricane season** runs from **June to November**, with the highest chance of storms in August and September. While this might sound scary, it's mostly a matter of monitoring the weather. If you visit outside those peak months, you're likely to enjoy quieter days in paradise with an unbeatable island calm.

In short, whether you're escaping the winter chill or seeking solitude in the summer, Tortola will be waiting with sunshine, smiles, and endless adventure!

Chapter 1. Brief History and Culture

Historical Background

Ah, Tortola — a place so steeped in history that every breeze feels like it's carrying whispers from centuries past. This island may seem like a peaceful paradise now, but its past is a swashbuckling tale of pirates, plantations, and power struggles that shaped the very soul of the British Virgin Islands.

Tortola's story begins long before European explorers set sail. The island was originally inhabited by the

Arawak and **Carib** peoples, who enjoyed the bounty of the land and sea for centuries. They thrived here, using the lush surroundings to hunt, fish, and craft pottery. However, in 1493, everything changed when **Christopher Columbus** arrived during his second voyage to the New World. While he didn't stay long, he did leave his mark, christening the chain of islands "Las Once Mil Vírgenes" — or **The Virgin Islands** — in honor of Saint Ursula and her 11,000 martyred virgins. Talk about making an impression!

Fast forward to the 1600s, when the British laid claim to Tortola, officially bringing it into their expanding empire. However, it wasn't long before the island's secluded coves and hidden bays became a haven for a very different crowd: **pirates**. Legendary swashbucklers like **Blackbeard** and **Captain Kidd** found refuge here, and rumors of hidden treasure still linger to this day. While you're more likely to stumble across a beach bar than buried loot, the adventurous spirit of Tortola's pirate past remains.

By the 18th century, Tortola had transitioned from pirate hideout to plantation economy, with sugar and cotton plantations thriving under British rule. Of course, this prosperity came at a great human cost — enslaved Africans were brought to the island to work the plantations, and their descendants still make up a significant portion of Tortola's population today. The island's culture and traditions are deeply influenced by African heritage, creating a vibrant and resilient community.

In 1834, **the British abolished slavery**, and Tortola's plantation economy declined. Over time, the island shifted its focus to fishing, farming, and — eventually — tourism. Today, Tortola stands as a testament to its layered history, from the ancient indigenous cultures to the colonial struggles and the enduring spirit of its people.

Local Traditions and Customs

Tortola may be a small island, but it's bursting with vibrant traditions and customs that reflect its unique blend of African, European, and Caribbean influences. One thing is for sure: Tortolans know how to celebrate life, and if you're lucky enough to visit during a festival, you're in for a treat.

One of the island's biggest and most beloved celebrations is the **BVI Emancipation Festival**, held every year in **August** to commemorate the abolition of slavery in 1834. This isn't your average holiday — it's an explosion of color, music, dancing, and, of course, incredible food. Picture this: streets lined with people in brightly colored costumes, steel bands playing infectious rhythms, and the scent of local delicacies like **Johnny cakes** and **roti** filling the air. It's a true carnival atmosphere, and everyone — locals and visitors alike — is invited to join in the fun. Don't be shy about showing off your dance moves; in Tortola, everyone's a dancer after a rum punch or two!

Another key aspect of Tortola's cultural fabric is its deep connection to the sea. The island's history as a pirate haunt and later a seafaring community has left its mark, and even today, you'll find a strong maritime tradition. Locals take pride in their sailing skills, and the island hosts several regattas throughout the year, most notably the **BVI Spring Regatta** in April. Whether you're a seasoned sailor or just want to watch the colorful sails dance on the horizon, this event is a nod to Tortola's enduring love affair with the ocean.

On a more day-to-day level, Tortolans are known for their warm hospitality. The island operates on **"island time"**, meaning things might not always run exactly on schedule — but that's part of the charm. Life moves at a slower, more relaxed pace here, and you'll quickly find yourself adapting to the rhythm. Don't be surprised if locals greet you with a friendly "Good morning" or "Good afternoon" — it's a small island, and acknowledging others is an important part of the culture. Manners matter in Tortola, so be sure to return the greeting!

Food, too, plays a central role in Tortola's traditions. Local dishes are often shared in a communal setting, whether it's a family gathering or a street-side cookout. Staples like **saltfish**, **fungi** (a cornmeal-based dish), and **callaloo** (a leafy green stew) are not just meals but cultural experiences that connect people to their African and Caribbean roots.

From festive parades to quiet moments shared over a plate of freshly cooked seafood, Tortola's traditions are a beautiful blend of history, community, and joy. As a visitor, you'll not only witness these customs but be welcomed to experience them firsthand — and trust me, by the time you leave, you'll feel like part of the family.

Language and Religion

Tortola may be a small island, but its language and religious landscape are as rich and diverse as the island itself. The official language spoken here is **English**, which is great news for most travelers — no need to brush up on your high school Spanish or practice saying "hello" in a dozen different ways. But hold on! Tortolans have their own unique way of speaking, often laced with a rhythmic, melodious Caribbean twist that makes even the most mundane conversations sound like a song. You'll quickly fall in love with the local **dialect**, where phrases like "Wha' happening?" (What's going on?) or "I good" (I'm fine) will become part of your island vocabulary.

But don't worry if you can't quite master the accent — the people of Tortola are incredibly welcoming and patient with visitors. They love to chat, share stories, and teach you a few local expressions. And who knows? By the end of your trip, you might be tossing around words like a true islander (just don't forget to drop that "r" sound!).

As for religion, **Christianity** is the predominant faith in Tortola, with most of the population belonging to various Christian denominations, particularly **Anglican, Methodist, Baptist**, and **Roman Catholic**. Churches are a central part of community life here, and it's not uncommon to hear the joyful sounds of gospel music spilling out into the streets on a Sunday morning. Even if you're not particularly religious, the spiritual energy in these services is infectious — you may find yourself swaying to the music, feeling the warmth of the community, and maybe even joining in a hymn or two.

Religion in Tortola is more than just a Sunday affair; it's woven into the island's fabric. Faith, family, and community go hand in hand, and this connection shows in the way locals live — with kindness, generosity, and a deep respect for the blessings they believe their island provides.

Chapter 2. Health and Safety Considerations

Health Care Services

When it comes to health care in Tortola, you'll be glad to know that while this island paradise may be far from the hustle and bustle of city life, it's not far from quality medical services. Now, no one likes to think about needing a doctor on vacation, but it's always good to be prepared — just in case you get a little too enthusiastic about diving, hiking, or, let's be honest, overindulging in those delicious beachside rum punches!

Tortola is home to the **Dr. D. Orlando Smith Hospital**, the island's main medical facility located in **Road Town**. It's a modern, well-equipped hospital offering a range of services, from emergency care to specialist consultations. The hospital can handle most routine and urgent medical needs, so if you happen to twist an ankle while hiking up Sage Mountain or get a jellyfish sting during a snorkel session, you'll be in good hands. The staff are professional and experienced, and you'll find that the warm Caribbean hospitality extends to the doctors and nurses, who treat everyone with care and kindness.

For minor issues, there are also several **private clinics** around the island, where you can quickly pop in for a check-up or to grab some medication if needed. Pharmacies are readily available too, with both local remedies and over-the-counter medicines you might recognize from home. Just remember, when island life is as carefree as Tortola's, things might run on "island time," so don't expect a 10-minute wait at all times — patience is key!

However, if you're traveling with any chronic conditions, it's a good idea to bring along any essential medications in sufficient quantities. While Tortola has reliable pharmacies, certain prescriptions might not be as easily accessible as back home. Travel insurance is also a smart idea, just to cover any unforeseen medical expenses.

Vaccination Requirements

The good news is that when it comes to vaccinations for Tortola, there's no need for any unusual or exotic shots before you land in paradise. If you're up to date on routine vaccines, such as **measles, mumps, rubella (MMR)** and the **seasonal flu shot**, you're pretty much good to go. Most travelers won't need any special vaccinations beyond what's typical for home, which is a relief if you're not a fan of needles!

However, the **Centers for Disease Control and Prevention (CDC)** does recommend that you make sure your tetanus-diphtheria-pertussis (Tdap) and

hepatitis A vaccines are up to date, just to be safe. Hepatitis A can be contracted through contaminated food or water, though the risk is generally low in Tortola. Still, it's better to be safe than sorry, especially if you plan to indulge in some adventurous street food or hit up a local beach BBQ (and trust me, you will!).

If you're a more intrepid traveler or plan on staying for an extended period, consider getting the **hepatitis B** vaccine, particularly if there's a chance of medical procedures or exposure to blood. Also, although there's no **yellow fever** in Tortola, if you're traveling from a country where yellow fever is a concern, you may be required to show proof of vaccination upon entry.

And of course, the most essential "vaccination" you'll need in Tortola is your daily dose of sunshine and relaxation — guaranteed to improve your mood and overall well-being! Just don't forget the sunscreen and mosquito repellent to keep yourself protected from sunburns and pesky bug bites while you're soaking up that glorious island vibe.

Safety Tips for Travelers

Ah, Tortola — where the most dangerous thing might just be getting too relaxed! But even in paradise, it's smart to keep a few safety tips in mind, just to ensure your trip stays as breezy as the island's trade winds.

First off, **Tortola is a safe place** to visit, and most travelers enjoy their time here without a hitch. That said, let's cover the basics: always use your common sense. Just because the island feels like one big hammock doesn't mean you should let your guard down completely. Keep an eye on your belongings, especially in busy spots like **Road Town** or popular beaches. Leave your valuables in your hotel safe, and try not to flash too much cash (though, let's be real, in

Tortola, your biggest splurge might be an extra piña colada).

When it comes to **transportation**, the island's winding roads can be an adventure of their own! If you're renting a car, remember that **Tortolans drive on the left** side of the road. Yes, it can be a bit disorienting at first — especially if you're used to driving on the right — but you'll get the hang of it. Just take it slow and be cautious on those tight mountain turns, where you might encounter a friendly goat or two!

As for **beach safety**, Tortola's waters are as inviting as they look, but always keep an eye on local warnings about currents or jellyfish. And while snorkeling is a must-do, make sure you're aware of your surroundings and avoid stepping on coral — both for your sake and the ocean's.

Finally, at night, stick to well-lit areas and travel in groups if possible. Tortola is incredibly peaceful, but a little extra caution never hurts.

With these simple tips in mind, you'll be all set to enjoy the island's beauty safely and happily!

Chapter 3. Currency, Payment Methods, and Tipping

Local Currency and Payment Methods

When it comes to spending your hard-earned cash in Tortola, you'll find that it's as easy as basking in the sun on a beach lounger. The local currency is the **East Caribbean Dollar (ECD),** which is a colorful and cheerful little bill that will make you feel like you're on a treasure hunt every time you pull out your wallet. The ECD is further divided into 100 cents, so if you find yourself counting coins, just remember: each one brings you closer to that next delicious conch fritter!

Now, let's get real — if you're coming from the U.S., you'll be pleased to know that the **U.S. Dollar (USD)** is also widely accepted on the island. This makes your life a whole lot easier, as you can simply use your familiar greenbacks without worrying about currency exchanges. Just be mindful that while you can pay with USD, your change may be given back in ECD, so don't be surprised if you find a mix of colorful bills in your pocket after a shopping spree at one of the local markets.

Payment Methods (Credit Cards and Cash)

When it comes to payment methods, Tortola is a blend of traditional and modern conveniences. Most hotels, restaurants, and shops accept major **credit cards** like Visa and MasterCard, making it easy to swipe your way through paradise. However, before you go on a shopping spree, do check with individual establishments, as some smaller vendors or local markets might only accept cash. Nothing's worse than finding the perfect souvenir and realizing your card won't do the trick!

If you're planning on exploring the charming local markets or grabbing a quick bite from a street vendor (and trust me, you don't want to miss out on the local delicacies), it's a good idea to have some cash on hand. ATMs are readily available in **Road Town**, so you can easily withdraw some local currency if you find yourself running low. Just remember, not all ATMs accept international cards, so have a backup plan or two — like making friends with a local who might be willing to lend you a few bucks for that incredible fish taco you spotted earlier!

While we're on the topic of cash, it's also worth noting that tipping is a customary practice in Tortola, as it is throughout the Caribbean. A tip of 15-20% is typical for good service in restaurants, and don't forget about those hardworking bartenders who keep your rum punches flowing! A couple of dollars for housekeeping at your hotel goes a long way, too, especially when you come back to a fresh towel animal greeting you after a long day in the sun.

Tipping Etiquette

Now, here's a little insider tip: While most restaurants add a service charge, it's always a good idea to double-check your bill to ensure you're not tipping twice. If you had a particularly memorable meal and the service was exceptional, feel free to add a little extra — those smiles and sunny attitudes deserve to be rewarded!

So, pack your bags, bring along some cash, and get ready to immerse yourself in the vibrant culture of Tortola. With the right currency and payment methods at your fingertips, you'll be free to enjoy all the sun, sand, and local flavors this Caribbean gem has to offer!

Chapter 4. How to Reach Tortola

International Flights and Airports

Ah, the thrill of air travel! The only time you get to experience both excitement and anxiety in a single moment — will your suitcase make it to Tortola, or will it be having a little adventure of its own in a distant land? Fear not, intrepid traveler! Tortola's **Terrance B. Lettsome International Airport (EIS)** is your gateway to paradise, and it's ready to welcome you with open arms (and possibly a refreshing rum punch).

EIS is located on **Beef Island**, just a short jaunt over a picturesque bridge from the main island of Tortola. While it might not be the biggest airport you've ever seen, it has all the charm of a Caribbean welcome. Once you step off the plane, the sweet scent of tropical flowers and the gentle breeze will envelop you like a cozy blanket, instantly melting away any travel-related stress.

Several major airlines offer flights to EIS from various cities in the United States and beyond, including American Airlines, Delta, and JetBlue. Keep an eye out for seasonal flights, as direct routes can vary. For those flying from the U.S., you can often find convenient connections through nearby islands like **St. Thomas** or **San Juan, Puerto Rico**. Just remember, if your flight is delayed, don't fret — it's all part of the island experience, and there's nothing a few minutes of staring at the crystal-clear water can't cure.

And speaking of connections, you may want to grab a local SIM card at the airport (or just rely on that trusty

Wi-Fi). Once you arrive, you'll want to share your arrival photos on social media, and what's a beach selfie without a geotag?

Ferry and Boat Services

Now, if you're feeling adventurous and want to experience the magic of island hopping, you're in for a treat! The **ferry and boat services** in the British Virgin Islands are as reliable as they are enjoyable. They provide a scenic way to reach Tortola from nearby islands, including **Virgin Gorda**, **Jost Van Dyke**, and **Anegada**.

The ferries are a delightful experience, offering breathtaking views of turquoise waters and lush green islands that will have you humming "Margaritaville" before you even step on board. Ferries typically run multiple times a day, making them a flexible option for your travel plans. Just be sure to check the schedule, as they can vary depending on the season and the day of the week. A little tip? Arrive early, grab a seat on the upper deck, and soak up those sun-kissed views while sipping a cold drink — it's the island way!

Once you're on the ferry, sit back and enjoy the ride, but hold on tight — that Caribbean breeze can whip your hair into a wild and untamed masterpiece! Keep your eyes peeled for dolphins and other sea life; they love to make an appearance, especially if you're waving a snack around.

If you're not in the mood for a public ferry, consider chartering a private boat. It might be a splurge, but imagine cruising through the turquoise waters with your loved ones, exploring hidden coves, and discovering secluded beaches that most tourists never see. Plus, you can set your own playlist and have the captain stop whenever you spot a particularly Instagrammable spot.

So, whether you're arriving via air or sea, the journey to Tortola is part of the adventure. Buckle up (or hold on tight) as you prepare to immerse yourself in the stunning beauty and vibrant culture of this Caribbean paradise!

Entry Requirements (Visas, Customs)

To enter Tortola, British Virgin Islands (BVI), here are the current requirements as of October 2024:

1. **Passport Validity**: Your passport must be valid for the duration of your stay, although it is recommended to have at least six months of validity remaining for international travel.

2. **Visa Requirements:**

   - **Visa-exempt Countries**: Visitors from the US, UK, Canada, and Schengen area do not require a visa for short stays (up to one month). However, an entry stamp will be issued upon arrival.

- **Visa Required Countries**: Nationals of certain countries may require a visa. If you hold a valid UK, US, or Canadian visa, you can enter the BVI for tourism or business for up to six months without needing a BVI-specific visa.

- You can apply for extensions beyond one month up to a total of six months if needed, and you may be asked to provide proof of financial means and accommodation plans.

3. **Other Requirements**:

- A return or onward ticket is required.

- An environmental levy of $10 USD is charged upon entry, and a departure tax of $50 USD is applied when leaving by air, or $20 USD if departing by ferry.

Make sure to check the specific visa requirements based on your nationality by contacting the BVI immigration authoritie

Chapter 5. Transportation Options

Getting Around Tortola

Welcome to Tortola, where the warm sun kisses your skin and the gentle breeze beckons you to explore! Now that you've arrived, you might be wondering how to get around this stunning island paradise. Fear not, for there are plenty of transportation options available to help you navigate your way to sun-soaked beaches and delectable dining spots.

First up, let's talk **taxis**. Taxis are a popular and convenient way to get around Tortola, and you'll find them ready and waiting at the airport, hotels, and popular attractions. They might not be the traditional yellow cabs you're used to, but these local taxis come in various shapes, sizes, and colors, giving you a taste of the island's personality. Most drivers are friendly and knowledgeable, often doubling as unofficial tour guides. So buckle up and get ready for some entertaining stories — just be prepared to possibly detour for a scenic view or two!

If you're feeling a bit more adventurous (and want to save some cash for those delicious rum cocktails), consider hopping on a local **bus**. The buses in Tortola may not be the sleekest of vehicles, but they're an experience you won't want to miss. These vibrant, open-sided buses have a quirky charm and a personality all their own. Plus, the fares are as low as your worries will be while lounging on the beach. Just flag one down, hop on, and don't be surprised if you end up making new friends during the ride. It's all part of the Tortola experience!

For the truly intrepid traveler, renting a car is another fantastic option. Imagine the wind in your hair as you drive along the island's scenic roads, with stunning views of the ocean on one side and lush mountains on the other. Just be prepared to take the wheel on the **left side of the road** — yes, that's right! Channel your inner James Bond and embrace the adventure.

Driving Tips and Road Conditions

Now, before you grab those car keys and set off on a joyride, let's chat about some important **driving tips and road conditions**. First and foremost, patience is key! The roads in Tortola are narrow and winding, and you'll encounter more than a few steep hills. Keep in mind that local drivers have mastered the art of navigating these roads, and they may zoom by you as if they're on a racetrack. Take it slow and enjoy the scenery — you're on island time now!

Also, watch out for **goats and donkeys**. Yes, you read that right! These lovable creatures have no concept of traffic rules and can pop up anywhere, turning a peaceful drive into an impromptu wildlife safari. So, keep your eyes peeled, and you might just find yourself smiling at a goat contemplating life by the roadside.

When it comes to road conditions, be prepared for some unexpected surprises. Potholes may be lurking around every corner, and the occasional loose gravel might test your driving skills. Just remember, it's all part of the adventure! If you can navigate your way through Tortola's roads, you'll earn bragging rights for the rest of your trip.

Lastly, be sure to fill up on gas before heading out for a day of exploration, as gas stations can be sparse in some areas. And don't forget to bring your sense of humor — because whether you're getting lost or enjoying the view, a good laugh is the best way to make memories on this island adventure!

So, grab your sunglasses, get behind the wheel (or hop in a taxi), and let the exploration of Tortola begin!

Ferries and Inter-Island Transportation

When it comes to exploring the breathtaking British Virgin Islands, don't just stay tethered to Tortola! It's time to set sail on the high seas and discover the beautiful neighbors that lie just beyond the horizon. Enter the charming world of **ferries and inter-island transportation** — your ticket to adventure and fun!

First up, let's talk about the ferries. They're not just a means of getting from point A to point B; they're a delightful journey in themselves! With several ferry services operating between Tortola and nearby islands like **Virgin Gorda**, **Jost Van Dyke**, and **Anegada**, you'll be whisked away across the sparkling turquoise waters, making you feel like the captain of your own ship. Imagine the wind in your hair, the sun on your face, and the thrill of spotting dolphins dancing in the waves. Just remember to hold on tight to your drink — you wouldn't want to lose a refreshing rum punch to the ocean gods!

Ferry schedules can vary, so it's a good idea to check ahead and plan your island-hopping adventure accordingly. Arriving early? Great! Grab a seat on the upper deck, soak in those panoramic views, and maybe even make some friends with fellow travelers. Who knows? You might find a buddy to share an unforgettable sunset with on a distant beach.

And if you're feeling a bit fancy, consider chartering a private boat. This way, you can set your own course and enjoy a personalized itinerary. Picture yourself gliding through the waves, stopping at hidden coves, and discovering secluded beaches that most tourists only dream about. Just remember, the only thing better than a beautiful island is the journey that takes you there! So grab your sunscreen and get ready for an unforgettable ride through paradise!

Chapter 6. Accommodations

Best Resorts and Hotels

Here are some of the top luxury resorts and hotels in Tortola, BVI, with current information:

1. **Scrub Island Resort, Spa & Marina**

    - Address: Scrub Island, off the east coast of Tortola
    - Phone: +1 284-394-3440

This luxurious private island resort features three secluded beaches, upscale hillside villas with private plunge pools, and a full-service marina. It offers an idyllic Caribbean escape, known for high-end service and tranquility.

Unique Feature: The resort is located on a private island, offering unparalleled privacy and access to multiple beaches.

Price Range: Starting from $600 per night

Opening Hours: Open year-round

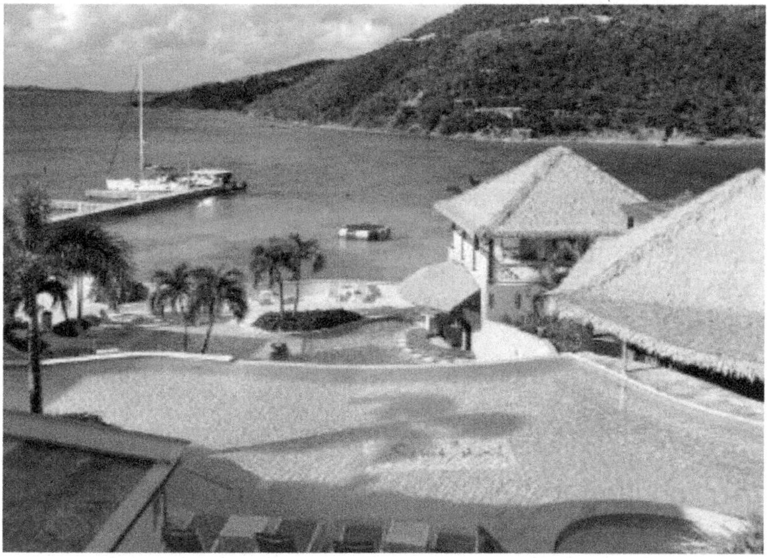

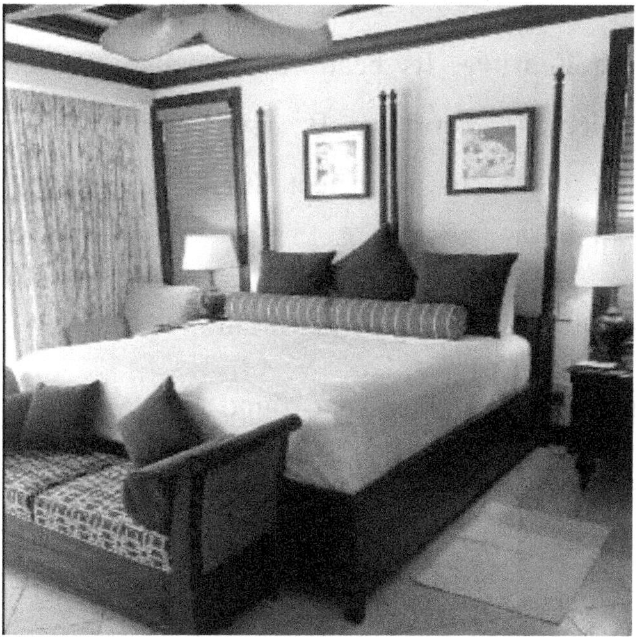

2. **Wyndham Tortola Lambert Beach Resort**

- Address: Lambert Beach, East End, Tortola
- Phone: +1 284-441-8070

Situated on over 14 acres of stunning beachfront, this resort combines tropical scenery with modern comforts. Guests can enjoy spacious suites, a large swimming pool with a swim-up bar, and dining at the Turtle Restaurant.

Unique Feature: Its beautiful, expansive beach and proximity to Terrance B. Lettsome International Airport make it a perfect blend of luxury and convenience.

Price Range: $300–$500 per night

Opening Hours: Open year-round

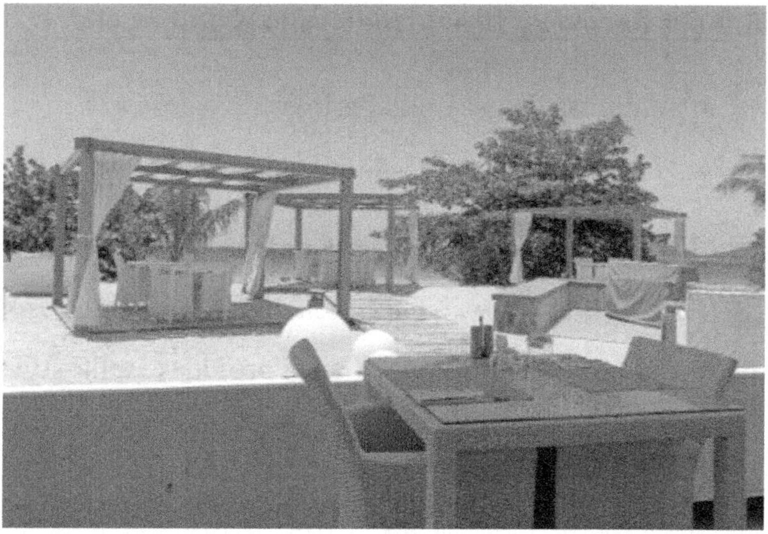

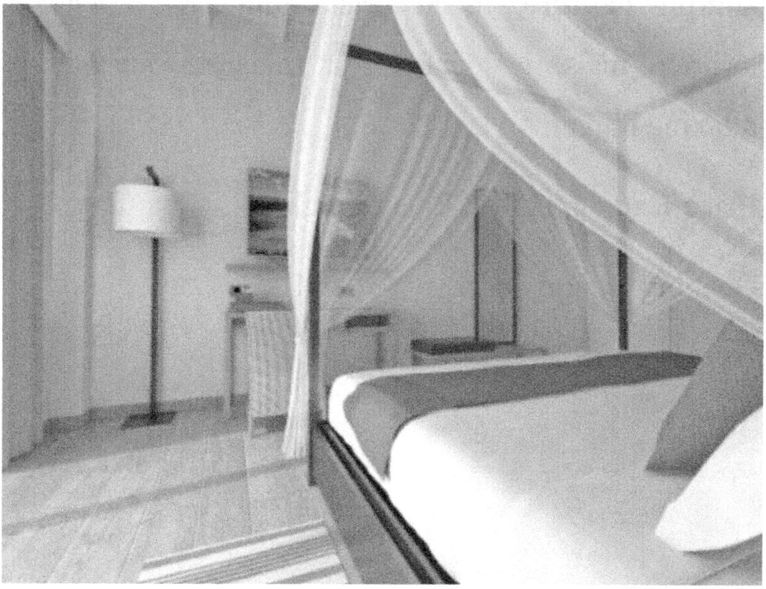

3. **Fort Recovery Beachfront Villa & Suites Hotel**

- Address: West End, Tortola
- Phone: +1 284-495-4466

Fort Recovery offers a unique blend of luxury and history. This beachfront hotel is set within a centuries-old fort and provides villa-style accommodations with private pools, as well as an on-site spa and wellness center.

Unique Feature: Its historic setting and beachfront location make it ideal for a romantic getaway or relaxing retreat.

Price Range: $350–$700 per night

Opening Hours: Open year-round

51

4. **Fort Burt Hotel**

- Address: Road Town, Tortola, British Virgin Islands
- Phone Number: +1 284-494-2587

Fort Burt Hotel is built on the remains of a 17th-century Dutch fort, offering a historic ambiance combined with modern comfort. It has 18 units, some with private pools. Guests can enjoy harbor views from balconies and an outdoor pool. Rooms are modest but clean, with some older furnishings. It's popular among pre- and post-cruise visitors due to its proximity to the marina and cruise pier.

Unique Feature: Historic setting with views of Road Town's harbor and an on-site fort structure.

Price Range: $99–$160 per night for standard rooms, $200–$385 for suites, depending on the season.

Opening Hours: Open year-round.

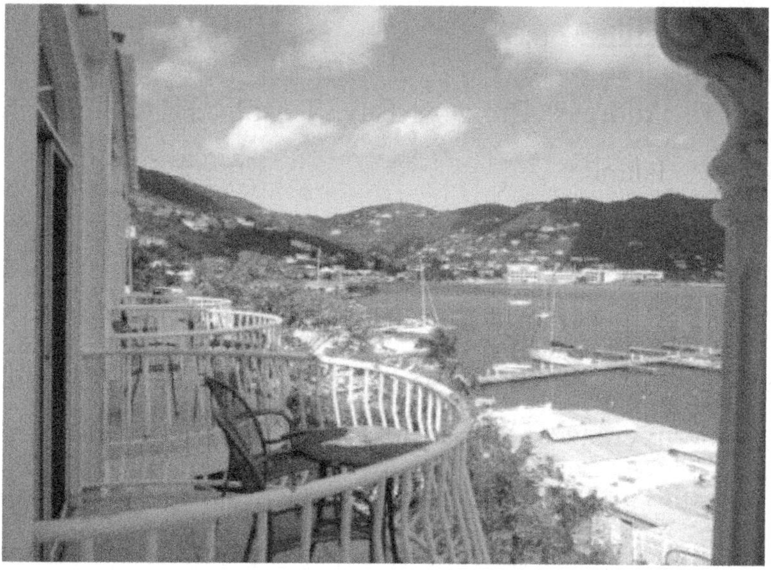

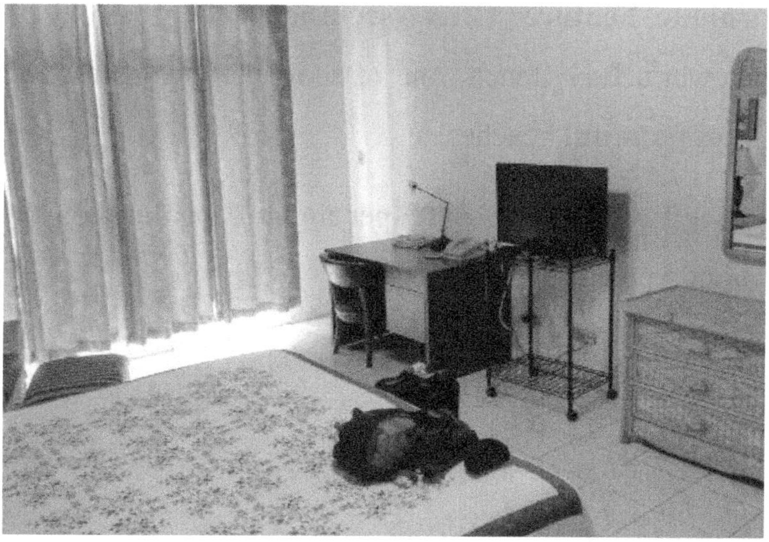

5. **Icis Villas**

- Address: Brewer's Bay, Tortola, British Virgin Islands
- Phone Number: +1 284-495-4224

Nestled in the lush surroundings of Brewer's Bay, Icis Villas is a peaceful retreat offering modern villas and cottages. The property is close to one of Tortola's most pristine beaches, and guests can relax in tropical gardens or enjoy the on-site restaurant and pool.

Unique Feature: Offers seclusion and proximity to Brewer's Bay Beach, one of the island's quietest and most beautiful beaches.

Price Range: $200–$400 per night, depending on the room type and season.

Opening Hours: Open year-round.

These accommodations combine luxury with unique features specific to Tortola's natural beauty and history.

Budget-Friendly Stays

Here are budget-friendly accommodation options in Tortola, BVI:

1. **Sebastian's on the Beach**

    - Address: Little Apple Bay, West End, Tortola, BVI

- Phone: +1 284-495-4212

This beachfront hotel offers comfortable rooms and suites with ocean views. It's a great spot for beachgoers and surfers, with an on-site restaurant serving Caribbean cuisine.

Unique Feature: Direct access to a popular surf beach.

Price Range: $125–$200 per night

Opening Hours: Open year-round

2. **Abigail's 2-Bedroom Apartment**

- Address: Road Town, Tortola, BVI
- Phone: Booking via Airbnb/Agoda

A cozy, fully equipped apartment ideal for budget-conscious travelers. It features a full kitchen and free Wi-Fi.

Unique Feature: Convenient central location and kitchen facilities for self-catering.

Price Range: $85–$150 per night

Opening Hours: Open year-round.

2. Heritage Inn

- Address: Windy Hill, Carrot Bay, Tortola, BVI
- Phone: +1 284-494-5842

Offering sweeping views of the ocean, this inn is known for its friendly atmosphere and outdoor pool. Rooms come with kitchenettes, making it convenient for longer stays.

Unique Feature: Amazing hillside views of the Caribbean Sea.

Price Range: Rates start from $135 per night.

Opening Hours: Open year-round with standard hotel check-in and check-out times.

3. Village Cay Hotel & Marina

- Address: Waterfront Drive, Road Town, Tortola, BVI
- Phone: +1 284-494-2771

Located in the heart of Road Town, this hotel is perfect for budget travelers looking for a central location. It offers marina views, a swimming pool, and an on-site restaurant.

Unique Feature: Easy access to the marina, perfect for boaters.

Price Range: Starting from $160 per night.

Opening Hours: Check-in from 2 PM, Check-out by 11 AM.

These accommodations provide comfort without breaking the bank while allowing you to explore the beauty of Tortola.

Chapter 7. Cuisine and Dining

Must-Try Dishes and Drinks

When in Tortola, your taste buds are in for an adventure as flavorful as the island itself! Get ready to savor the **vibrant Caribbean cuisine**, where every bite feels like a celebration of the island's culture and history. From mouthwatering seafood to signature cocktails, the culinary scene in Tortola is an experience you won't forget.

First up, if you're a seafood lover, you're in paradise! Be sure to try the **conch fritters**. These deep-fried delights are crispy on the outside and tender on the inside, with chunks of fresh conch mixed into a savory batter. Pair them with a tangy dipping sauce, and you'll feel like you've struck gold. And don't miss the chance to sample **freshly caught lobster**, especially during lobster season! Grilled to perfection with garlic butter and a hint of island spices, this dish is a symphony of flavors that'll have you singing its praises.

For something a little heartier, dig into **roti**. This dish, inspired by Indian flavors, features a flatbread stuffed with curried meats or vegetables. It's the kind of meal that wraps you up in warmth and comfort — much like the island itself. And for the ultimate in local comfort food, try **fish and fungi** (not the mushroom kind!). Fungi is a cornmeal-based side dish similar to polenta, and it pairs perfectly with stewed fish for a truly authentic Caribbean meal.

Now, let's talk drinks. The island's signature drink is, of course, **rum**. You can't leave Tortola without sipping on a classic **painkiller**, a creamy concoction of rum, pineapple juice, orange juice, and coconut cream, topped with a sprinkle of nutmeg. One sip, and you'll understand how it got its name — it's like stress melts away with every delicious gulp.

And for something refreshing, try the locally made **Ting** soda. This fizzy, grapefruit-flavored drink is a zesty wake-up call for your taste buds and the perfect companion for a sunny day.

Whether you're indulging in Tortola's seafood or sipping on its famous cocktails, every meal here is a feast for the senses!

Best Restaurants and Local Eateries

Here are some of the best restaurants and local eateries in Tortola, BVI, with current and up-to-date details:

1. **Capriccio di Mare**

    - Address: 2 Admin Dr, Road Town, Tortola
    - Phone: +1 284-494-5369

A popular Italian trattoria near the cruise port, known for its espresso, gelato, fresh pasta, and pizza. It's a cozy, casual spot with outdoor seating that captures the essence of a traditional Italian café.

Unique Feature: The turquoise Vespa outside and the authentic Italian menu in the heart of Tortola.

Price Range: $$

Opening Hours: 9 AM – 9 PM

2. **Island Tacos**

- Address: Pier Park, Road Town, Tortola
- Phone: +1 284-541-7989

A grab-and-go spot located in a red shipping container. It offers a delicious selection of tacos, burritos, and Mexican-style salad bowls, perfect for a quick bite. Popular among locals and tourists alike.

Unique Feature: Vibrant, budget-friendly eatery with great food for visitors at the pier.

Price Range: $

Opening Hours: 11 AM – 5 PM

3. **Banana's Restaurant**

- Address: Cane Garden Bay, Tortola
- Phone: +1 284-341-2260

This beachfront restaurant is a go-to for those looking to try local food. With large portions and Caribbean-inspired dishes, the setting is as stunning as the flavors. Don't miss the local Bushwacker cocktail!

Unique Feature: Its beachfront location, making it ideal for a meal with a view of Cane Garden Bay.

Price Range: $$

Opening Hours: 12 PM – 10 PM

4. The Sugar Mill Restaurant

Address: Sugar Mill Hotel, Apple Bay, Tortola

Phone: +1 284-495-4355

A renowned fine dining restaurant at the Sugar Mill Hotel. Known for its romantic ambiance and top-tier menu, including lobster and risotto dishes.

Unique Feature: Romantic seaside setting with views of Apple Bay, perfect for a special dinner.

Price Range: $$$

Opening Hours: 6 PM – 10 PM (Dinner Only)

5. **J Blakx Food Truck**

- Address: Waterfront Drive, Road Town, Tortola
- Phone: +1 284-540-2122

A food truck specializing in barbecue dishes, including brisket and jerk chicken. It's perfect for a quick but satisfying lunch. Delivery options are available as well.

Unique Feature: Convenient and budget-friendly BBQ spot near the Governor's House.

Price Range: $$

Opening Hours: 11 AM – 4 PM

These options provide a range of local and international cuisine, from quick bites to fine dining, ensuring something for every palate in Tortola.

Capriccio di Mare
GELATO
Banana Split
Chocolate Nut Sundae
...or just by the scoop!

Chapter 8. Practical Information

Emergency Contacts and Medical Services

Alright, let's be real for a moment — while no one plans to have an emergency while vacationing in paradise, it's always good to be prepared. But hey, don't worry! Tortola has you covered in case of any mishaps, from minor sunburns to "I-tried-surfing-and-now-I'm-in-a-cast" situations.

First and foremost, if you need help in an emergency, dial **911** for police, fire, or medical assistance. It's a straightforward number, even if you're still groggy from too many painkillers (the drink, not the meds!) the night before. But here's a pro tip: while Tortola's emergency services are responsive, island time is a real thing. So, if you can, avoid needing to call 911 by staying hydrated, wearing sunscreen, and not getting too adventurous on those steep mountain hikes!

When it comes to **medical services**, Tortola offers several options for health care. The main facility is **Peebles Hospital**, now known as the **Dr. D. Orlando Smith Hospital**, located in the capital, Road Town. It's modern and equipped with the essentials, so whether you've taken a tumble off a paddleboard or had a little too much sun, they've got you sorted. For less urgent matters, there are also several private clinics and pharmacies scattered around the island. And don't fret — medical professionals in Tortola are well-trained, and most speak English fluently, which is great when you need to describe how that snorkeling mishap really went down.

Be sure to bring **travel insurance** that covers medical expenses, especially if you plan on doing any adventurous activities. It'll give you peace of mind knowing that should you run into trouble, you won't need to sell your left kidney to cover hospital fees!

Internet, Mobile Connectivity, and SIM Cards

We all know that staying connected is a must, whether it's to update your Instagram with envy-inducing beach pics or to assure your loved ones back home that you're "surviving" in paradise. Thankfully, Tortola's got your back when it comes to **internet and mobile connectivity**.

Most hotels, resorts, and cafes offer **Wi-Fi**, though the speed can sometimes be as slow as a lazy island afternoon. If you're uploading vacation pics, expect it to take a little longer than you're used to — but hey, just think of it as a forced digital detox! For the more remote areas of the island, Wi-Fi might be harder to come by, so it's worth considering a backup plan.

For those who need to stay connected 24/7 (because heaven forbid you miss that work email), getting a **local SIM card** is the way to go. You can easily purchase one from local providers like **Flow** or **Digicel** at the airport, in Road Town, or at retail outlets around the island. Pop it into your unlocked phone, and you'll be surfing the web like a local in no time. Plans usually offer a combination of data, calls, and texts, so you won't have to worry about those international roaming fees giving you a heart attack.

Coverage on the island is generally good, but you may hit a few dead spots when driving through the mountains or venturing to secluded beaches. But honestly, if you're on a hidden beach in Tortola, do you really need to be checking your messages? Put the phone down, grab a coconut drink, and enjoy the island life.

In summary, whether you're calling for backup or just posting vacation bragging rights online, Tortola has all the essentials for staying connected and safe — just with a little island flair!

Local Laws and Etiquette

When visiting Tortola, it's always a good idea to familiarize yourself with a few local laws and customs so you don't accidentally turn your island escape into a cautionary tale. While Tortola is laid-back, there are some rules you'll want to follow to avoid any "whoops" moments with the local authorities.

First things first: **driving under the influence** is a big no-no. Yes, you're in rum paradise, but if you've indulged in one too many painkillers (the drink, not the meds), don't even think about getting behind the wheel. The local police take drunk driving seriously, so plan on taking a taxi after a night of Caribbean cocktails.

Another thing to remember is that **public nudity** (and topless sunbathing) is a definite faux pas. While you might feel tempted to embrace your inner free spirit on Tortola's pristine beaches, keep your swimsuit on — even when the sun is scorching. The locals tend to be more conservative in this regard, and going au naturel could land you in some awkward situations.

Speaking of attire, when you're wandering through the towns or stopping for a bite to eat, it's considered respectful to cover up. **Walking around in just your swimsuit** might be fine for the beach, but it's seen as impolite when you're off the sand. A simple cover-up or a shirt and shorts will do, and you'll blend right in.

Now, let's talk about the golden rule of island life: **respect the locals**. A smile, a friendly greeting, and good manners will go a long way in Tortola. You'll often hear the phrase "good morning" or "good afternoon" from locals, and it's customary to return the greeting. And when it comes to photography, always ask permission before snapping a picture of someone — especially in more rural areas where people value their privacy.

Language Tips for Travelers

English is the official language of the British Virgin Islands, so you won't have to scramble to find your translation app while in Tortola. But, as with any destination, learning a few local phrases and tips can help you connect with the island's culture — and perhaps even impress the locals!

First off, while English is spoken, the **accent** can sometimes throw you for a loop, especially if you're not used to the Caribbean's melodic, fast-paced style. The locals tend to speak with a distinct Virgin Islands dialect that blends a little Caribbean flair into the Queen's English. You might need to listen carefully at first, but once you tune into the rhythm, you'll feel right at home.

Here's a fun phrase to learn: **"Limin'"**. It's a quintessential island term meaning "hanging out" or "relaxing." If a local asks you if you're "limin'," they're not offering you a citrus fruit — they just want to know if you're chilling out and enjoying the vibe. And trust me, limin' is something you'll be doing a lot of in Tortola.

While not as common as English, some locals also speak **Creole**, a mix of African, European, and Caribbean languages. Don't worry too much about mastering Creole — just being aware of it will deepen your appreciation for the island's culture.

One more tip: always remember to greet people warmly. Saying **"good morning"** or **"good afternoon"** before starting a conversation is customary and shows respect. So, don't rush straight into your questions — take a moment to acknowledge the person with a friendly greeting. The locals will appreciate your effort and, who knows, you might just earn yourself a new island friend!

So, while English will serve you well on Tortola, sprinkling in a bit of local charm and etiquette will make your island experience all the sweeter!

Chapter 9. Must-See Attractions

Cane Garden Bay

Cane Garden Bay is the kind of place that looks like it jumped straight off a postcard and landed right into your vacation dreams. Imagine the quintessential Caribbean paradise: a crescent-shaped stretch of powdery white sand, calm, crystal-clear waters that gently lap the shore, and palm trees swaying lazily in the breeze. It's no wonder Cane Garden Bay is often hailed as **Tortola's crown jewel**, and once you set foot here, you'll understand why.

One of the first things you'll notice is the water. Oh, the water! It's like nature mixed up the perfect batch of blues, blending aquamarine, turquoise, and sapphire into a liquid masterpiece. This bay's calm waters make it an ideal spot for **swimming, paddleboarding, and snorkeling**. Whether you're a water sports enthusiast or just someone who enjoys floating around like a starfish, Cane Garden Bay has you covered.

For those with an adventurous spirit, **rent a kayak or a paddleboard** and head out to explore the gentle waves. You might even encounter some friendly marine life, like sea turtles or colorful fish darting through the coral below. But if your version of adventure is more about soaking up the sun and sipping on something cold, Cane Garden Bay is equally perfect for that too. There's a reason why this spot is popular with families, couples, and solo travelers alike: it strikes that perfect balance between relaxation and activity.

Speaking of sipping, let's not forget the **beach bars**. Cane Garden Bay is home to some of Tortola's most iconic watering holes, where you can cool off with a refreshing cocktail or sample some local rum (it would be rude not to!). Don't leave without trying a famous **rum punch**, made with the finest island spirits and guaranteed to make you feel like a true islander. As the sun starts to dip toward the horizon, the atmosphere here becomes even more magical. Grab a drink, find a cozy spot on the sand, and prepare for a sunset that will leave you speechless. The sky lights up in hues of pink, orange, and gold, turning the bay into a dreamy landscape.

And if you're lucky enough to visit during the evening, Cane Garden Bay often comes alive with **live music** and a vibrant atmosphere. Local bands play everything from reggae to calypso, filling the night air with island rhythms that are impossible to resist. Before you know it, you'll be dancing in the sand, barefoot, drink in hand, and grinning from ear to ear. It's a vibe, and it's infectious.

But Cane Garden Bay isn't just about the beach and the drinks (although, let's be honest, those are pretty great). It's also about the people. The locals who live and work around the bay are warm, welcoming, and full of stories. You'll find beachside vendors selling handmade crafts, and you can even have a chat with the fishermen who bring in their daily catch. It's these small moments of connection that make a visit here so special.

In summary, Cane Garden Bay is the kind of place that makes you forget all your worries. Whether you're swimming in the clear waters, sipping on a cocktail, or just lying on the sand soaking in the sun, time seems to slow down here. It's Tortola at its finest: laid-back, beautiful, and brimming with that magical island charm. Just don't blame us if you never want to leave!

Smuggler's Cove

If there's a hidden gem in Tortola that's been whispering secrets to the wind for centuries, it's Smuggler's Cove. This beach, tucked away at the far western end of the island, is like the island's best-kept secret — except the secret's out, and you're about to be let in on the magic. Smuggler's Cove is the definition of off-the-beaten-path, and trust me, it's worth every twist and turn on the bumpy road to get there. When you finally arrive, it feels like you've discovered your very own slice of paradise — no treasure map required.

As you step onto the beach, you'll be struck by the pristine beauty of the place. Smuggler's Cove is refreshingly untouched by development, with no massive resorts or loud beach bars in sight. Just nature doing its thing, and doing it exceptionally well. The sand is a soft, golden blanket beneath your feet, and the water? Let's just say it's the kind of blue that makes you wonder if someone turned up the saturation in real life. It's calm, clear, and perfect for a lazy swim or a bit of snorkeling.

Speaking of snorkeling, this is one of the best spots on Tortola to experience **underwater life**. Grab your gear and head out into the shallow waters, where you'll be greeted by schools of colorful fish darting around coral formations. If you're lucky, you might even spot a sea turtle cruising through the waters like it owns the place (spoiler alert: it does). Smuggler's Cove offers an intimate snorkeling experience where the sea creatures are your only companions, and there's something magical about feeling like you're the only one in on the secret.

What really sets Smuggler's Cove apart from other beaches is the **sense of tranquility**. It's quieter here, more secluded, and it feels like the world slows down the moment you arrive. There's no rush, no crowds, no agenda — just you, the beach, and the gentle rhythm of the waves. It's the kind of place where you can finally crack open that novel you've been meaning to read or take an epic nap under a palm tree, lulled by the sound of the ocean.

Now, here's a fun tidbit: the beach gets its name from its **pirate past**. Legend has it that, back in the day, Smuggler's Cove was a favorite hideout for pirates and smugglers who used its secluded shores to stash their loot. So while you're basking in the sun, you can daydream about buried treasure and pirate ships (or at least pretend that your sunscreen bottle is a hidden doubloon).

But fair warning: getting to Smuggler's Cove requires a little bit of effort. The road leading to the beach can be an adventure in itself, especially if it's been raining.

It's a bumpy, unpaved path, but that's all part of the charm. Plus, once you arrive and see the stunning, untouched beauty before you, all thoughts of the rugged drive will disappear faster than you can say "arr matey!"

In a nutshell, Smuggler's Cove is for those who want to get away from it all and enjoy the natural, quiet beauty of Tortola. It's perfect for snorkeling, swimming, or simply doing nothing but soaking in the serenity. If you're looking for an authentic, unspoiled beach experience with a dash of pirate lore, this hidden gem will steal your heart. Just be prepared: once you've spent a day at Smuggler's Cove, no other beach might ever measure up!

Sage Mountain National Park

If you've ever dreamed of hiking through a lush tropical forest while feeling like you've stepped into a scene from Jurassic Park (minus the dinosaurs, of course), then **Sage Mountain National Park** is your paradise. Rising majestically 1,716 feet above sea level, Sage Mountain is the highest point in all the British Virgin Islands, offering not only a refreshing escape from the beach but also sweeping views that will leave you in awe.

Let's start with the drive to get there. As you ascend the winding roads of Tortola, you'll notice the temperature start to drop ever so slightly, and the landscape transforms from coastal beauty to vibrant greenery. It feels like you're being drawn into a secret world, far from the hustle and bustle of everyday life. When you finally reach the entrance to **Sage Mountain**, you'll quickly realize that this is a whole new side of Tortola — one where nature reigns supreme.

Now, Sage Mountain isn't your typical Caribbean experience. Instead of palm trees and sandy shores, you'll find yourself surrounded by a dense forest of mahogany trees, ferns, and vines that drape elegantly over the path, like nature's own chandelier. This is a slice of tropical rainforest, with towering trees creating a shady canopy and the scent of fresh earth filling the air. The chirping of birds and rustling of leaves are your soundtrack as you begin your hike through this lush oasis.

There are several trails to choose from, all of varying difficulty levels. For the more adventurous, the **hike to the summit** is a must. Don't worry, it's not Everest-level intense, but be prepared for a bit of a workout. The reward? Breathtaking panoramic views that stretch across Tortola and the neighboring islands, all the way to the U.S. Virgin Islands on a clear day. It's the kind of view that makes you stop in your tracks, take a deep breath, and simply appreciate the sheer beauty of this planet. Trust me, the Instagram likes are a bonus — the real joy comes from soaking in the serenity of it all.

For those looking for a more leisurely experience, the shorter **circular trail** around the base of the mountain is just as magical. As you stroll through the forest, it's hard not to feel a sense of calm wash over you. The lush vegetation, combined with the occasional burst of colorful tropical flowers, creates a sensory overload in the best way possible. Plus, there's a good chance you'll spot some wildlife — keep your eyes peeled for birds like the rare **BVI parrot** or even a mongoose darting through the underbrush.

And don't worry if you're not an expert hiker. The trails are well-marked, and the park is small enough that you won't get lost (unless you're really committed to losing yourself in nature, of course). Whether you're an experienced adventurer or just looking for a peaceful walk in the woods, Sage Mountain has something for everyone.

One of the coolest things about Sage Mountain National Park is that it's a reminder of Tortola's rich natural history. Much of the island was once covered in dense forests like this, and the park serves as a living time capsule of what the island's landscape used to look like. It's a chance to step back in time, long before the days of beachfront resorts and rum cocktails, and experience the raw, untamed beauty of the Caribbean.

So, if you're ready to swap the beach for the mountains (at least for a few hours), Sage Mountain National Park is calling your name. Lace up your hiking shoes, pack a water bottle, and prepare to be wowed by Tortola's wild side. Just don't forget your camera — the views from the top are legendary, and you'll want to capture every moment of this unforgettable adventure.

Road Town (Capital City Highlights)

Welcome to **Road Town**, the bustling heart and soul of Tortola! As the capital city of the British Virgin Islands, Road Town might be small in size, but it's packed with character, charm, and a lively Caribbean vibe that's hard to resist. Here, island life meets modern convenience, with a sprinkle of history and culture thrown in for good measure. Whether you're strolling through its colorful streets, exploring the waterfront, or diving into its rich past, Road Town is where the island's pulse beats strongest.

Let's start at the **Waterfront Drive**, where the city hugs the shores of the sparkling Caribbean Sea. This is the perfect place to take a leisurely walk, breathe in the salty sea air, and watch the ferries and yachts glide in and out of the harbor. There's something almost meditative about the way the boats sway in the marina, and if you're lucky, you might catch a glimpse of a luxury yacht that looks more like a floating mansion. Hey, it's the Caribbean — anything can happen!

If you're a history buff (or just someone who appreciates a good story), Road Town won't disappoint. A visit to the **J.R. O'Neal Botanic Gardens** is a must. Not only is it a lush, tropical haven in the heart of the city, but it's also steeped in local history. Wander through its carefully curated paths and marvel at exotic plants, fragrant orchids, and towering palm trees. It's the perfect place to escape the city's heat and enjoy a quiet moment with nature — plus, the flowers make for some seriously Instagram-worthy photos.

For a deeper dive into the island's past, **the 1780 Lower Estate Sugar Works Museum** is the place to go. This restored sugar mill tells the story of Tortola's colonial history, from the sugar industry to the days of slavery. It's a sobering reminder of the island's past, but also a fascinating glimpse into how the BVI has evolved over the centuries. The stone ruins and old machinery are hauntingly beautiful, and as you wander through, it's impossible not to reflect on the resilience and strength of the people who built this place.

If you're more of a **shopping enthusiast**, Road Town's got you covered, too. Head over to **Main Street**, where the city's commercial heart beats. Here, you'll find everything from local boutiques selling handmade crafts to duty-free shops with Caribbean rums and perfumes that will leave you smelling like a tropical breeze. Keep an eye out for locally made souvenirs — whether it's a hand-carved wooden sculpture, vibrant batik fabrics, or locally harvested spices, you're sure to find something that captures the spirit of the islands.

Feeling peckish after all that exploring? Road Town's **culinary scene** is as diverse as its people. Whether you're craving fresh seafood, hearty Caribbean fare, or international cuisine, the city's restaurants and street vendors serve up a feast of flavors. Try the local delicacy of **conch fritters** or dive into a plate of juicy jerk chicken with a side of plantains. And whatever you do, don't skip dessert — the island's rich coconut and pineapple-based sweets will leave your taste buds dancing.

Of course, no visit to Road Town would be complete without a stop at the **Crafts Alive Village**, a vibrant market where local artisans display their creations. This colorful collection of stalls is a treasure trove of handmade jewelry, paintings, textiles, and all things uniquely Tortolan. Whether you're shopping for a keepsake or just browsing, it's a great way to support local artisans and take home a piece of the island's creativity.

In a nutshell, Road Town is the perfect mix of past and present, offering visitors a chance to soak up Tortola's rich history, vibrant culture, and laid-back Caribbean charm. It's a place where the pace of life slows down, the people greet you with a warm smile, and there's always something new to discover around every corner. Whether you're sipping a coffee by the harbor or getting lost in the history of the sugar plantations, Road Town is a city that will stay with you long after you've left its shores.

Brewer's Bay

If you're searching for a beach in Tortola that feels like a blissful secret hidden away from the world, **Brewer's Bay** is calling your name. Nestled on the north side of the island, this serene stretch of sand is the ultimate spot for those who prefer tranquility over tourist crowds, and palm trees over parasols. It's the kind of place that makes you feel like you've just stumbled upon a deserted paradise—except there are no deserted pirates, just you, the sea, and a sense of pure relaxation.

The journey to Brewer's Bay is an adventure in itself, as you wind your way through Tortola's lush hills and along curving roads with jaw-dropping views of the ocean below. As you descend into the bay, you'll immediately sense that this place is different. Brewer's Bay isn't trying to be the next big thing—it's just happily existing in its own peaceful bubble, untouched by the rush of modern life. And that's what makes it so special.

Once you step onto the soft, golden sands, you'll feel an immediate calm wash over you. Unlike some of Tortola's busier beaches, Brewer's Bay is often delightfully quiet, with only a handful of fellow beachgoers around. This is the kind of place where you can spread out your towel, take a deep breath, and let the gentle lapping of the waves lull you into the perfect state of island bliss. It's a beach made for lazy days—so settle in and prepare to do absolutely nothing, and love every second of it.

One of the biggest draws of Brewer's Bay is its **snorkeling**. Grab your mask and fins, and head into the crystal-clear waters where you'll be greeted by vibrant coral reefs and an array of tropical fish. You don't have to swim far from shore to be immersed in the underwater wonderland—schools of blue tangs and parrotfish glide effortlessly through the water, and if you're lucky, you might spot a friendly sea turtle gracefully cruising by. The shallow reefs make this spot perfect for both beginners and seasoned snorkelers alike, so whether it's your first time or your fiftieth, Brewer's Bay has something magical in store.

But it's not just the underwater world that makes Brewer's Bay stand out. The bay is steeped in **history**, too. Back in the day, this area was home to a rum distillery, hence the name "Brewer's Bay." While you won't find barrels of rum lying around (sadly), you can still see remnants of the old plantation and distillery if you venture inland. It's a reminder of the island's past, tucked away behind the tropical foliage like a well-kept secret waiting to be discovered.

If you're feeling peckish after a swim, Brewer's Bay is home to a few cozy beachside eateries where you can grab a bite. Picture yourself munching on freshly grilled fish while gazing out at the turquoise sea—a true Caribbean dream come true. And don't forget to wash it down with a refreshing rum punch, because, well, you're in the BVI, and rum is practically a way of life here.

Brewer's Bay is more than just a beach—it's an experience, a place where time slows down, and the only thing on your agenda is to soak up the natural beauty surrounding you. Whether you're snorkeling among colorful fish, lounging under the shade of a swaying palm, or simply basking in the peacefulness of it all, Brewer's Bay is guaranteed to capture your heart.

So, if you're craving a day of relaxation and quiet adventure, Brewer's Bay is the perfect escape. It's a little slice of heaven where the worries of the world melt away, and all that's left is the sound of the sea and the warmth of the sun on your skin. Pack your snorkel, grab a good book, and get ready to fall in love with Tortola's best-kept secret.

Chapter 10. Activities and Adventures

Snorkeling and Diving Spots

If Tortola's stunning coastline is the icing on the cake, then its underwater world is the gooey, irresistible center. Whether you're a seasoned diver or just someone who enjoys floating above the reef with a snorkel in hand, Tortola's **snorkeling and diving spots** are nothing short of magical. Imagine swimming through crystal-clear waters, gliding past vibrant coral gardens, and crossing paths with exotic marine life.

Welcome to Tortola's watery wonderland, where every dive feels like uncovering a hidden treasure.

One of the top spots for snorkeling and diving is **Smuggler's Cove**, a place that, aside from its intriguing name, boasts some of the clearest waters and most vibrant coral reefs on the island. Slip on your snorkel and mask, and suddenly you're face to face with schools of tropical fish, darting through intricate coral formations. It's like stepping into a real-life aquarium, only without the glass walls. Keep an eye out for parrotfish, angelfish, and even sea turtles, which seem to glide by as if they own the place (and honestly, they do).

For a dive that's more on the legendary side, there's **The RMS Rhone**, one of the Caribbean's most famous shipwrecks and a must-do for diving enthusiasts. This British mail ship sank during a hurricane in 1867, and today, its remains rest on the sea floor, offering an unforgettable dive site. As you explore the rusted relic, you'll feel a mix of excitement and eerie calm, like you're diving back in time. Don't be surprised if you spot barracudas or giant groupers hanging around the wreck like they're guarding some sort of underwater museum. It's a dive that will leave you in awe — and with plenty of epic tales to tell back on land.

Another gem is **Brewer's Bay**, perfect for both novice and experienced snorkelers. Here, the water is so clear you can practically see the fish waving at you before you even jump in. The coral formations are pristine, and the calm waters make it ideal for a leisurely snorkel. If you're a fan of underwater photography, this is your spot — the visibility is unreal, and the marine life is happy to pose for a few snapshots.

Boating, Sailing, and Yachting

Ah, Tortola — where the sea breeze is your best friend, and the waves invite you to sail off into the sunset like some sort of swashbuckling adventurer (minus the pirates). **Boating, sailing, and yachting** are not just activities here; they're a way of life. Whether you're a seasoned sailor or a first-time yachter, the waters surrounding Tortola offer some of the most scenic and peaceful sailing experiences in the world.

First off, you can't talk about sailing in Tortola without mentioning **The Sir Francis Drake Channel**. This picturesque stretch of water between Tortola and its neighboring islands is a sailor's dream — calm seas, a steady breeze, and panoramic views that seem straight out of a postcard. You'll sail past uninhabited islands, hidden coves, and beaches so pristine you'll wonder if you've somehow sailed into a fantasy novel. The best part? You can drop anchor and take a swim wherever you please — no crowded tourist traps here.

For those who like their adventures with a bit more luxury, yachting in Tortola is a must. Imagine lounging on the deck of a sleek, modern yacht, sipping a tropical drink as the wind gently tousles your hair. This isn't just sailing; it's the ultimate form of relaxation. Charter a yacht for the day (or week, if you're really treating yourself) and explore the British Virgin Islands in style. Visit secluded beaches, snorkel in hidden coves, and enjoy a sunset that seems to have been painted just for you. Whether you're celebrating a special occasion or simply living your best life, yachting in Tortola is pure bliss.

But if you're more of a hands-on adventurer, rent a sailboat and take the helm yourself. Tortola's consistent trade winds and calm waters make it a fantastic spot for sailors of all levels. Beginners can take a lesson or two, while seasoned pros can set sail and explore the countless islands and islets scattered around. It's freedom on the water, with nothing but the horizon ahead and the sound of the waves lapping at your boat.

So, whether you're gliding over the coral reefs or sailing into the sunset, Tortola's waters are a playground for the adventurous at heart. Grab your snorkel, hoist the sails, and prepare for a journey that will leave you with memories as colorful as the fish you'll encounter.

Hiking Trails and Nature Walks

Tortola isn't just a paradise for beach lovers; it's also a haven for hikers and nature enthusiasts. With its lush mountains, stunning vistas, and winding trails, the island offers some of the most picturesque hiking spots in the Caribbean. So lace up those hiking boots and get ready to sweat a little—your reward will be jaw-dropping views and perhaps a few friendly iguanas along the way.

One of the top trails to conquer is the **Ridge Road**, a scenic path that promises to deliver panoramic views of the island and the surrounding sea. As you ascend, the world below unfolds like a stunning watercolor painting, with greens, blues, and whites blending together in a beautiful mosaic. Just keep in mind that this hike is more than a leisurely stroll; you'll work up a sweat, and you might even question your life choices about three-quarters of the way up. But fear not! The views from the top will have you shouting "I'm on top of the world!" or at least feeling like a heroic explorer who's just discovered a new land.

For those who prefer their hikes a bit more off the beaten path, the Tortola Rainforest Trail is your answer. This lush, tropical trail leads you through a dense forest filled with towering trees, colorful flowers, and maybe even a parrot or two squawking above your head. Along the way, keep your eyes peeled for the fascinating local wildlife—think of it as a live-action version of a nature documentary, except without David Attenborough narrating your every move. The cool shade provided by the canopy makes this hike a little more forgiving, and the sweet smell of nature is an invigorating reminder that there's more to Tortola than just sunbathing.

And let's not forget about the National Park Trails, where you can immerse yourself in the island's biodiversity. With trails that vary in difficulty, there's something for everyone, from leisurely walkers to hardcore hikers. You'll encounter hidden waterfalls, rocky cliffs, and plenty of Instagram-worthy photo ops. Just be sure to take a moment to appreciate the tranquility of nature; after all, it's not every day you get to feel like you're in a real-life postcard.

Water Sports (Kayaking, Paddleboarding)

If you thought the fun stopped once you left the beach, think again! Tortola is a playground for water sports enthusiasts, and it's time to get your splash on with **kayaking and paddleboarding**. Picture yourself gliding over the calm, turquoise waters, feeling like a sea captain on a quest for treasure. Spoiler alert: the only treasure you'll find is pure joy and perhaps a few starfish along the way.

Kayaking is one of the best ways to explore Tortola's stunning coastline. Rent a kayak and paddle your way around the hidden coves and secluded beaches that are just waiting to be discovered. If you're lucky, you might even encounter a curious sea turtle or a playful dolphin joining you for a portion of your journey. As you paddle through the clear waters, the sights and sounds of the sea create a beautiful soundtrack, and you might find yourself humming along to the rhythm of the waves. Just remember to steer clear of the rocky areas unless you fancy a new adventure in the form of a minor kayak mishap!

For those who prefer a more zen-like experience, **paddleboarding** is the way to go. It's the perfect blend of tranquility and fitness, allowing you to engage your core while floating on the water like a graceful sea otter. Stand up, paddle out, and take in the breathtaking views of Tortola's coastline. If you're feeling adventurous, challenge yourself to balance while you take the obligatory selfie—you'll either come away with a stunning photo or a hilarious story of your near plunge into the water.

Tortola's waters are calm and welcoming, making both kayaking and paddleboarding accessible for all skill levels. Plus, you'll have a front-row seat to the island's breathtaking beauty—so get out there, paddle away your worries, and make some unforgettable memories on the water. Whether you're navigating through mangroves, exploring the shoreline, or simply soaking up the sun, Tortola is ready to show you an aquatic adventure that you won't soon forget!

Chapter 11. Shopping and Local Markets

Souvenir Shops and Local Crafts

Ah, the quest for the perfect souvenir! It's an age-old tradition that involves a mix of love, a sprinkle of desperation, and a dash of "What on earth will I do with this?" When you're in Tortola, the souvenir shops and local crafts are not just places to empty your wallet; they're treasure troves filled with memories waiting to be found. So, roll up your sleeves and prepare to embark on an adventure that's just as exciting as any day spent on the beach.

Let's start with the local craft shops, where artisans pour their heart and soul into every piece. Here, you can find everything from hand-painted ceramics to intricate jewelry that would make even the most seasoned fashionista green with envy. Imagine stumbling upon a vibrant, handwoven basket that screams, "Take me home and make your living room look fabulous!" Or a piece of locally crafted jewelry that becomes your new favorite accessory and the perfect conversation starter at parties. "Oh this? I got it in Tortola. You've probably never heard of it."

For a truly unique experience, seek out the **Tortola Handicraft Cooperative**, where local artisans showcase their finest work. You'll find everything from wooden carvings to colorful textiles that tell stories of the island's rich culture. Plus, it's an opportunity to meet the talented creators behind these beautiful pieces—don't be surprised if you find yourself engaged in a lively conversation about the history of the island while contemplating which item truly deserves to be your "I was here" trophy.

Don't forget to keep an eye out for the whimsical coconut crafts, which range from decorative bowls to intricate sculptures. Who knew coconuts could be so artistic? It's hard not to chuckle when you find a coconut carved to resemble a happy face; it's like bringing a bit of Tortola cheer back home with you.

Popular Markets for Local Goods

Now, if you're ready to dive into the heart of Tortola's local culture, the bustling markets are where the real magic happens. Forget about sterile shopping malls; here, the vibrant energy and colorful stalls are your ultimate playground. The most famous of them all is the **Road Town Market**, where you can immerse yourself in the local way of life while hunting for that one-of-a-kind gem.

As you stroll through the market, your senses will be treated to an explosion of sights, sounds, and scents. Fresh fruits and vegetables overflow from stalls, creating a colorful mosaic that's both beautiful and mouth-watering. Try not to drool over the array of exotic fruits you've never even heard of—like sapodilla or guava—while simultaneously bargaining for the best price. Just remember, haggling is part of the fun, and you might find that the vendors are just as entertaining as their goods!

The Road Town Market is also home to a variety of local spices, herbs, and homemade condiments that'll make your taste buds dance with joy. Ever thought of taking a taste of Tortola back home? Grab a jar of local hot sauce, and soon your friends will be begging for a taste of "that spicy stuff" you brought back from your adventures.

If you're in search of some genuine handmade crafts, **the Craft Market** is another gem worth exploring. It's like stepping into a treasure chest filled with unique finds, from colorful clothing and handmade jewelry to intricately designed home decor. The artisans here pour their love and creativity into their crafts, and purchasing their work feels like supporting a piece of Tortola's soul.

So, whether you're hunting for the perfect coconut sculpture or bargaining for the best deal on fresh local produce, Tortola's souvenir shops and markets offer a delightful blend of culture, creativity, and community. Embrace the joy of shopping, savor the laughter shared with local vendors, and leave with not just souvenirs but stories to tell and memories to cherish. Because in Tortola, every purchase is more than just an item; it's a slice of island life wrapped up with a bow of joy!

Chapter 12. Sample Itineraries

Family-Friendly Itinerary (3-5 Days)

Planning a family vacation to Tortola? Buckle up, because this island has the perfect balance of relaxation, adventure, and a touch of chaos (the good kind). From building sandcastles to snorkeling, your family will make enough memories to last a lifetime—or at least until the next vacation!

Day 1: Settle in & Hit the Beach

After arriving in Tortola and shaking off that "travel mode" feeling, head straight to **Cane Garden Bay**. This iconic beach is the perfect introduction to Tortola's sandy goodness. Picture it: kids squealing as they jump into the gentle waves, parents lounging on the shore pretending to read while secretly nodding off. Spend the afternoon swimming, building sandcastles, and indulging in some local snacks. Maybe let the kids bury you in the sand for that ultimate "parent of the year" moment.

Day 2: Nature Walks & Animal Encounters

Start the morning with a family hike at **Sage Mountain National Park**. The kids will love spotting wildlife along the trails, and you'll get to enjoy breathtaking views. It's an educational experience disguised as fun—win-win! For lunch, grab a bite at a local beach café before heading to **Brewer's Bay** for some afternoon snorkeling. The shallow waters are perfect for beginners, and who knows, your little ones might just spot their first sea turtle!

Day 3: Pirate Day & Cultural Fun

What's a trip to the Caribbean without a little pirate action? Hop aboard a family-friendly **pirate boat tour**, where the kids can pretend to be swashbuckling adventurers, while you enjoy the scenery (and maybe sneak a rum punch). After your pirate escapades, spend the afternoon exploring **Road Town**. Visit the local craft markets to pick out some fun souvenirs (a seashell necklace, perhaps?), and treat the kids to some delicious island ice cream.

Day 4: Island-Hopping Adventure

Take a **ferry to nearby islands**, like Jost Van Dyke or Virgin Gorda, for a fun day of exploring new beaches and more snorkeling adventures. It's a great way to mix things up and feel like you're globe-trotting (well, island-hopping) without straying too far from Tortola.

Day 5: Relax & Recharge

For your final day, slow things down. Return to your favorite beach or spend some time enjoying **water sports** like paddleboarding or kayaking. Wrap up the trip with a sunset cruise—it's the perfect way to say goodbye to Tortola, with the sea breeze in your hair and your heart full of unforgettable family memories.

Adventure Seeker's Itinerary (3-5 Days)

If you've come to Tortola for adventure, get ready for a whirlwind of action-packed days that'll have you living life on the edge (safely, of course). This itinerary is all about adrenaline, thrills, and maybe a few "Did I really just do that?" moments. Let's dive in!

Day 1: Hiking and High Views

Start your adventure with a morning hike up **Sage Mountain National Park**. At 1,716 feet, it's the highest peak in the Virgin Islands, and the trek up will get your heart pumping. The trails wind through lush rainforest, and when you reach the top, you'll be greeted by panoramic views that make every drop of sweat worth it. Your reward? The bragging rights of hiking Tortola's toughest trail and an Instagram shot that'll make everyone back home jealous.

After the hike, cool off by heading to **Smuggler's Cove** for some beachside relaxation—or, more likely in your case, some vigorous swimming or body surfing. Smuggler's Cove is a hidden gem with fewer tourists and more space to let your adventurous spirit roam free.

Day 2: Watersports Extravaganza

Ready to hit the water? Spend today trying out **kayaking** and **paddleboarding** at **Cane Garden Bay**. After you've mastered standing on the paddleboard without wiping out (hey, no judgment here), take things up a notch with some **windsurfing** lessons. You'll feel like a superhero gliding across the water with the wind at your back.

By the afternoon, trade your paddle for a mask and fins, and dive into the vibrant underwater world with **snorkeling** at **Brewer's Bay**. Keep an eye out for colorful fish, coral reefs, and maybe even a stingray gliding by.

Day 3: Sailing and Island Hopping

No adventure in Tortola is complete without sailing. Charter a boat for the day and explore the surrounding islands, like **Jost Van Dyke** or **Norman Island**, rumored to be the inspiration for "Treasure Island."

Snorkel in hidden coves, cliff dive (if you dare), and let your inner pirate roam free on the open seas.

Day 4: Diving Deep

For the ultimate underwater adventure, book a **scuba diving** excursion to explore Tortola's famous dive sites, like the wreck of the **RMS Rhone**. Descend into the depths and marvel at the eerie, awe-inspiring beauty of this historic shipwreck—perfect for both seasoned divers and adventurous newbies.

Day 5: Extreme Watersports & Farewell Fun

Wrap up your trip with some serious thrills: **jet skiing** or even **parasailing** for those adrenaline junkies who want a bird's-eye view of the island. Finish with a sunset cocktail cruise—a well-earned relaxation after days of pure adventure.

Cultural and Historical Itinerary (3-5 Days)

For those who crave stories of the past and a deep dive into local traditions, Tortola's cultural and historical treasures will leave you spellbound. This itinerary is perfect for soaking up the island's rich heritage while exploring its most iconic sites. Expect history, heart, and maybe a little time travel.

Day 1: Road Town's Cultural Gems

Start your journey in **Road Town**, the bustling capital and the heart of Tortola's history. Begin with a visit to the **Virgin Islands Folk Museum**, a tiny but fascinating spot packed with artifacts that paint a picture of the island's colonial past, slavery era, and maritime history. You'll feel the weight of the stories that shaped this beautiful land—don't forget to ask the museum staff for their favorite local tales!

Afterward, stroll down the historic streets and make your way to the **Old Government House Museum**. This beautifully restored colonial building gives you a peek into the island's political past and offers stunning views of the harbor. Grab lunch at a local café, where the conversations flow as easily as the sea breeze.

Day 2: Annaberg Plantation Ruins

Time to step further back in history with a visit to the **Annaberg Plantation Ruins**. Although technically on **St. John**, it's just a quick ferry ride away and worth every second. This former sugar plantation tells the somber yet essential story of the island's enslaved laborers and the once-booming sugar trade. The views from the ruins are breathtaking, and the energy of the place is profound. Take your time walking through the old structures and imagining life during the plantation's peak.

Day 3: Callwood Rum Distillery & Local Crafts

Head to **Callwood Rum Distillery**, one of the oldest rum distilleries in the Caribbean, for a taste of history in liquid form. Sip on some locally produced rum, made using centuries-old methods, and learn about the island's distilling traditions that date back to the 18th century.

End your day browsing through **local craft markets** in Road Town or Cane Garden Bay. These markets are alive with the island's artistic spirit, from vibrant paintings to handcrafted jewelry, offering a wonderful taste of Tortola's culture to take home with you.

Day 4: Historical Hikes

Spend the morning hiking through Sage **Mountain National Park**. While this may seem like just another scenic walk, the park holds historical significance as it's been preserved since colonial times. Its lush forests and panoramic views evoke the island's deep connection with nature, which has been central to its history.

Day 5: Cultural Events & Local Music

If your timing is right, don't miss out on **Tortola's cultural festivals**—the BVI Emancipation Festival being one of the most vibrant. Experience the island's lively traditions through music, dancing, and delicious food that'll give you a true taste of Tortola's cultural soul. If festivals aren't happening, catch some live local music at a beach bar to end your trip on a joyful note, with rhythms that reflect Tortola's beating heart.

Conclusion

Final Thoughts

As your journey through Tortola comes to an end, it's clear that this island is more than just a tropical getaway—it's a place where history, culture, adventure, and relaxation collide in the most breathtaking ways. Whether you found peace on the pristine beaches, excitement in the turquoise waters, or a deeper connection through its rich history and vibrant traditions, Tortola has a way of leaving its mark on your heart.

Every corner of the island tells a story, and by exploring it, you've now become a part of that story too. So, whether this was your first visit or one of many, we hope that Tortola will always call you back with open arms and warm sea breezes.

Polite Request for Feedback or Reviews

We sincerely hope this guide has helped make your Tortola adventure unforgettable. Your feedback is incredibly valuable to us! If you found this guide useful, informative, or even just a good read, we would be honored if you could take a moment to leave a positive review or share your thoughts. Your feedback not only helps us improve but also assists future travelers in making the most of their own trips. Thank you for choosing this guide, and we wish you safe and happy travels wherever your next adventure takes you!

Made in the USA
Middletown, DE
29 December 2024